THE WEA~
OF (
WARI

Volume 4

"For Teens"
And Young Adults

Kenneth Scott

All Scriptures in this publication are taken from the King James version of the bible or paraphrased by the author.

The Weapons Of Our Warfare is a registered trademark of Spiritual Warfare Ministries, Inc., Birmingham, Alabama.

First Edition of Volume 4

The Weapons Of Our Warfare volume 4

Copyright © 2002 by Spiritual Warfare Ministries, Inc.

Spiritual Warfare Ministries
Attention: Kenneth Scott
P.O. Box 2024
Birmingham, Alabama 35201-2024

(205) 853-9509

(For the weapons of our warfare are not carnal, but mighty through God to the pulling down of strong holds;) Casting down imaginations, and every high thing that exalteth itself against the knowledge of God, and bringing into captivity every thought to the obedience of Christ.

2 Corinthians 10:4-5

Contents

Contents Continued

Dedication:

This book is dedicated to my loving, darling daughter, Angela Renae Scott. She has been a blessing to my life from birth, and I am truly thankful to the Lord for her.

"Introduction"

When Jesus was just twelve years old, His (earthly) parents took Him on a trip to Jerusalem which they took every year to attend the Passover. After the Passover, they began their journey home along with many others. They thought that Jesus was among the many family members, friends, and relatives that made this journey with them. But after about a day's journey, they looked for Jesus but could not find Him.

They then began a frantic search for Him and backtracked their journey all the way to Jerusalem. They finally found Him three days later in the temple teaching the biblical doctors, scribes, and scholars. When Mary found Him, she asked, "why did you do this terrible thing," meaning, having them so worried and afraid for Him. Jesus answered Mary and said, *"...didn't you know that I must begin doing my Father's business."*

The scripture goes on to say that Mary and Joseph

didn't understand what He meant by this. I believe that what Jesus meant by this was that the age of twelve years old signified a new stage in His life, whereby it was time for Him to begin doing the will of God.

When the Bible notes what seem to be small details, they are actually not small details at all. God didn't have to note Jesus' age when this happened. But he noted it for a very important purpose. I believe that His purpose was to show us that the age of twelve begins the age of spiritual accountability.

As teenagers, your parents are "physically" responsible for you until you get 18 years of age. This is one of the reasons why it is so important for you to give them respect and honor. It's important because, until the age of 18, they are responsible for making provisions for you, teaching and training you, and thereby are ultimately responsible for your actions.

This however, was an age that was set and established by our society. It is a good age because it has been proven that in our modern day society, 18 is the age that most young men and women begin to mature and become responsible. Some learn maturity and responsibility a lot earlier, and unfortunately, some a lot later. However, as a rule of thumb, 18 is the average age. But this age is only the age of responsibility to society. Because there are two areas of responsibility and accountability to which we all must answer. One is our responsibility and accountability to society, and the other is our responsibility and accountability to God.

I believe that God was showing us through this biblical account with Jesus, that the age of twelve is the age whereby He begins to hold you responsible for your   actions. It's the age at which you are going to be responsible for, and answer to God for your sins, disobedience, and transgressions against Him. Now, even though spiritual maturity sometimes takes longer than physical maturity, twelve is the be- ginning age of which God begins to hold you ac- countable.

With this in mind, if you are going to be spiritually responsible for your actions beginning at twelve, this must also become the age in which you being equip- ping yourself spiritually.

> *For we wrestle not against flesh and blood, but against principalities, against powers, against the rulers of the darkness of this world, against spiritual wickedness in high places.*
>
> *Ephesians 6:12*

As a young Christian, you must understand that you are in a type of spiritual war against Satan and evil spirits. It is Satan's desire to keep you from re- ceiving Christ if he can. But if he can't, his next plan is to wage war against your spirit and attempt to lure you into as much sin, disobedience, and iniquity as he can. His goal is that if he cannot stop you from becoming a Christian altogether, he wants to keep you as a carnal, worldly, and ineffective Christian.

> *Wherefore take unto you the whole armour of God, that ye may be able to withstand in the evil day, and having done all, to stand. Stand therefore, having your loins girt about with truth, and having on the breast-plate of righteousness. And your feet shod with the preparation of the gospel of peace. Above all, taking the shield of faith, wherewith ye shall be able to quench all the fiery darts of the wicked. And take the helmet of salvation, and the sword of the Spirit, which is the word of God: praying always with all prayer and supplication in the Spirit, and watching thereunto with all perseverance and supplication for all saints.*
>
> *Ephesians 6:13-18*

This passage of scripture goes on to say that if you are going to have any success in winning this war against Satan and evil spirits of sin and disobedience in your life, you are going to have to equip yourself with your spiritual armor.

Your spiritual armor consists of many things, but primarily of prayer and the Word of God. It's through hearing the Word, praying the Word, and confessing the Word, that you will be able to ulti-mately obey the Word. Without it, you will fall victim to Satan and the forces of darkness that fight against you and tempt you.

This book, "*The Weapons of Our Warfare Volume 4*" is a book of many prayers that will help you in your warfare against Satan and evil sprits that war against you. There are prayers for just about every situation you will face as a young man or woman of God.

As a young Christian, you may not be developed in prayer, and may not know the scriptures you need to combat the devil in your life. But God has anointed us with this book to aid and assist you in prayer. These prayers are filled with and comprised totally of the Word of God.

As you pray these prayers, God will help and strengthen you in your Christian walk. The more you pray them, the more you will learn scripture and learn how to pray on your own. You may also purchase *"The Weapons of Our Warfare Volume 3"* to help you with scripture and confessions. Now, prepare yourself for battle, as you experience, "*The Weapons of Our Warfare Volume 4, For Teens and Young Adults*."

Chapter I

Prayers of Praise, Thanksgiving and Daily Prayers

Prayer of Thanksgiving and Praise

Heavenly Father, as I come before You this day, I give You all the glory, honor, praise, adoration, and thanksgiving.

I thank You for loving me so much, that You gave Your only begotten Son, Jesus Christ to die on the cross for me; and I thank You for giving me salvation and eternal life through Him.

I thank You for Your grace, Your goodness, Your loving kindness, and Your tender mercy towards me.

I give You praise and thanksgiving for waking me up this morning and giving me life today. I thank You for giving me a good and sound mind, and for blessing me today with my health and strength.

I thank You for my family, and for blessing me with parents who love me, care for me, and work hard to provide for me.

I thank You for blessing me with my home, and for blessing me with food, clothing, and all of Your many wonderful blessings and provisions in my life.

I thank You for blessing me with my friends, family, and schoolmates.

I thank You for blessing me with: (*name other things you are thankful for*).

As You have blessed my life and the lives of my family, I pray that You would also bless others who are less fortunate.

Father, Your Word says, in all things give thanks; so I give You all the thanksgiving, glory, honor, and praise for these, and all of Your many wonderful blessings in my life.

In the name of the Lord, Jesus Christ, I pray. AMEN!

Scriptures Used In This Prayer:

Samuel 22:50
1 Chronicles 16:34
Psalms 92:1
Psalms 100:4
Psalms 106:1
1 Thessalonians 5:18
Matthew 6:13

A Daily Prayer

Our Father in heaven, I come boldly before You this day in the name of our Lord, Jesus Christ, praying for my day.

Father, I pray for Your wisdom this day, and that You would lead, guide, and direct me throughout my day—at home, school, and every place that I go.

I pray for Your provisions, blessings, and divine favor to be upon my life this day. And I pray that You would bless me to prosper and have good success in every area of my life.

I pray that You would bless me to walk in good health, and that You would not allow any sickness or disease to come upon me, or even come near me.

I pray that You would help me to have a close walk with You this day, as well as every day of my life. Help me to walk in obedience to Your Word and Your ways. And help me to walk in truth, integrity, and honesty with my parents, family, friends, and all those with whom I come in contact.

I pray that You would cover me this day with Your anointing, presence, and Your power.

I pray that You would keep me from sin and from wrongdoing. Keep me from disobeying You or Your Word, and keep me from disobeying my parents, and others in authority over me.

I thank You Father for assigning Your angels to make a hedge around me this day. I confess Your Word that they watch over me in all my ways to keep me from all hurt, harm, and danger. I thank You that Your angels are also assigned to keep all of my family members safe from any accidents, hurt, harm or danger.

As a child of God, I bind and loose every evil spirit from my life this day, and from the lives of my family, by the authority of God in the name of Jesus Christ.

Now Father, I commit this day unto You. And I thank You that Your goodness and mercy shall follow me throughout this day, and every day of my life.

In the name of the Lord, Jesus Christ, I pray. AMEN!

Scriptures Used In This Prayer:

Hebrews 4:16
Psalms 31:3
Psalms 1:3
3 John 1:2
Psalms 91:10
James 4:8
Galatians 5:16
Jude 1:24
Matthew 6:12
Psalms 91:11-12
Matthew 16:19
Psalms 37:5
Proverbs 16:3
Psalms 23:6
Psalms 23:6

A Confession of
"The Lord's Prayer"

Our Father, which is in heaven—holy, blessed, and glorious is Your name. Your kingdom (which is Your power and authority) has come unto us. Therefore, I speak Your Word, that Your will is done on earth—and in my life, as it is done in heaven.

I bind and loose Satan's will of killing, stealing, and destruction from being performed and carried out in my life. Instead, I decree that only the will of God (God's abundant life, prosperity, and blessings) is carried out in my life.

I pray that You would give me this day my daily bread. I thank You for my daily bread of healing and good health, safety, prosperity, and Your many blessings and provisions in my life.

I ask for forgiveness for my wrongs and sins, and I ask that You would also forgive those who have wronged or sinned against me. Help me not to be lured or lead into temptation, and deliver me from every snare of Satan, and from every one of his evil attacks against me.

For Yours is the Kingdom, the power, and the glory, forever and ever, AMEN!

Scriptures Used In This Prayer:

Matthew 6:9-13

Chapter II

Prayers for Your Parents, School, Church, and Our Nation

For Your Parents

F ather, I come before You this day thanking You for my parents, and lifting them up before You in prayer.

Father, even as You love us, I pray that You would cause my parents to always love You, and serve You with all of their heart, soul, strength, and might.

I pray for Your wisdom and Your hand of guidance and direction to be upon my parents. May You lead, guide and direct them by Your Spirit in every path they take. I pray that You would also divinely lead and guide my parents in every decision they make concerning their jobs, business, our home, and every aspect of their lives and our family.

I pray that You would help me to love, honor, re-spect, and obey my parents. Help me not to think evil or wrong of them, and help me not to be rebellious against them. For Your Word says that this is pleas-ing unto You, and You will (because of my obedience to Your Word) bless me with a long, healthy, and prosperous life.

I pray that You would protect them each and every day. May You place Your angels in a hedge around my parents to watch over them, protect them, and keep them safe from all accidents, hurt, harm and danger.

I pray that You would keep them from all evil, and may You also deliver them from each and every trick, trap, and snare of Satan.

I bind and loose every evil and demonic spirit that would attempt to come against my parents by the authority of the name of Jesus Christ. I decree according to the Word of God that no weapon (spiritual or physical) that is formed against them can prosper in any way, and every evil spirit that rises against them shall be rebuked.

I pray for Your power, presence, and anointing to be upon my parents, and may You keep them in good health—healed by the stripes of Jesus Christ.

I pray for Your blessings of prosperity and favor to be upon my parents. May You bless them with promotions, advancements, and good success upon their jobs, and in every area and aspect of their lives.

Now Father, I commit my parents to You this day. And as I have prayed Your Word over them, I am thankful that You are faithful to watch over Your Word to perform it in their lives.

In the name of Jesus Christ, I pray. AMEN!

Scriptures Used In This Prayer:

1 John 4:19
Mark 12:30
James 1:5
Psalms 37:23
Ephesians 6:1-3
Psalms 91:11-12
Matthew 6:13
Matthew 16:19
Job 22:28
Isaiah 54:17
Isaiah 10:27
Joshua 1:8
Psalms 1:3
Psalms 37:5
Jeremiah 1:12

For Your School

F ather, I come before You this day lifting up my school, (*name of Your school*) in prayer.

I pray that You would watch over us and keep us safe while we are traveling to and from school (*whether we walk or ride by bus or car*).

I pray that You would give the teachers in my school a genuine heart of conviction, love, and compassion to teach and love each and every student. May You give them the wisdom of God, and the knowledge, skill, and understanding they need to effectively teach each student in a manner which will enable us to learn and retain the information we are taught.

I pray that Your angels would watch over our school, and every student in our school—keeping us safe from all violence, hurt, harm, and danger.

Father, I pray that You would expose and reveal any student with intentions to harm or hurt others. And I confess Your Word that no weapon (physical or spiritual) that is formed against us can prosper in any way.

I bind every evil and demonic spirit from our school. I decree that every evil and demonic power, presence, and influence is off limits to our school, every student, teacher, and staff in our school, and is helpless and powerless to prosper against us.

Father, I pray that You would cover my school and everyone in my school with Your presence, power, and Your anointing. May You bring salvation to those who are not Christians, and draw each and every student, teacher, and staff close to You each day.

I pray that Your blessings would be upon every student, teacher, and staff member of my school. And, may You also bless us to prosper in academics, activities, sports, and in every other area.

Now, Father, as I have prayed for my school, I confess that Your Word (which I have prayed) cannot return to You void, but it shall accomplish that in which I have prayed for on behalf of my school.

In the name of Jesus Christ, I pray. AMEN!

Scriptures Used In This Prayer:

Proverbs 18:10
James 1:5
Exodus 31:3
Psalms 91:4
Psalms 91:11
Matthew 16:19
Malachi 3:11
Isaiah 54:17
Psalms 91:4
2 Peter 3:9
James 4:8
Numbers 6:24-26
Psalms 1:3
Isaiah 55:11

For Church Services

Father, I come before You this day lifting up my church service before You in prayer.

I pray that You would bless and anoint each and every part of the service, and each and every person who would take part in this service. I pray that You would bless and anoint the praise and worship leaders, the choir, the musicians, the ushers, and everyone who serves in any way in this service today.

I pray that Your anointing, presence, and power would rest upon our pastor/youth-teacher to bring us Your Word. I pray that as he/she comes to teach Your Word, may You speak through them, and use them to bring forth the message today with clarity and understanding.

I pray that You would bless each of us to be attentive to the speaker, and to the teaching of Your Word. Bless us to receive personal insight and understanding in Your Word. May You help us to hide Your Word in our hearts, and to apply it to our lives, so that we may become doers of Your Word, and not hearers only.

Father, I pray that You would draw every backslider and every person who is unsaved or not born-again to You. As the altar call is given, I thank You for drawing them by Your Spirit to true repentance, salvation, and deliverance. I pray that You would not only draw the unsaved and backslider, but that You would draw each of us closer to You, and may You also draw new members to our church.

I bind every evil spirit that would attempt to hinder this service, hinder our pastor/youth-teacher from bringing forth the Word, or hinder anyone from receiving the Word. I decree every evil spirit to be helpless, powerless and ineffective to bring any hindrance or disruption to this service in any way.

Now Father, I commit this service unto You. I pray that You would be highly exalted through this service. As we leave this service today, bless each and every person to leave changed in their heart, mind, and soul. And, bless each person to also leave charged, strengthened, and encouraged in Christ Jesus.

In the name of Jesus Christ, I Pray, AMEN!

Scriptures Used In This Prayer:

Isaiah 10:27
Psalms 150:1-6
1 Corinthians 2:4
2 Timothy 2:21
Exodus 31:3
Nehemiah 8:3
Proverbs 2:6
Psalms 119:11
James 1:22
Acts 2:47
Matthew 3:8
Matthew 9:13
Matthew 16:19
Job 9:12
Isaiah 54:17
2 Corinthians 10:4
Psalms 37:5
James 4:10
1 Samuel 30:6
Colossians 1:10-11

For our Nation and Leaders

F ather, You instructed for us to pray for and lift up our nation and those who are in authority. So in obedience to Your Word, I pray for, and lift up our nation and our leaders.

I lift up our community leaders, mayor and city leaders, governor and state officials, our president, his cabinet, and all those who are instrumental in the leading of our community, city, state, and our nation.

Father, I pray that You would give them divine guidance, direction, instruction, and counsel. I pray that the Spirit of the Lord would rest upon them with godly wisdom and knowledge, and that You would help them and give them solutions to the problems and affairs of our community, city, state, and our nation.

Your Word says that if Your people would humble themselves and pray, then You would deliver us, and heal our nation. Father, I humble myself and pray on behalf of this nation for the healing of our land. I pray that You would heal and deliver us from the problems of crime, violence, drugs, and other problems that plague our land.

I pray that You would guard and protect us from terrorism, sabotage, and every evil plot against this nation, and against the people of this nation. I speak Your Word that no weapon that is formed against this nation can prosper in any way, and I bind and loose every evil and satanic weapon that is formed or set against us.

Father, Your Word says, "Blessed is the nation who acknowledges You as Lord." Father, I confess and acknowledge that You are God, and that Jesus Christ is still Lord of the United States of America. I pray that You would always be Lord of our nation, and that You would draw the hearts of the people of our nation closer to You.

Now Father, I pray that You would continue to shower Your blessings of protection, prosperity, and abundance upon us. And I pray that Your goodness and mercy shall continue to rest upon us, and keep us (as a nation) in all our ways.

In the name of Jesus Christ, I pray, AMEN!

Scriptures Used In This Prayer:

1 Timothy 2:1-2
Psalms 37:23
Exodus 31:3
Isaiah 11:2
2 Chronicles 7:14
Psalms 91:3-6
Psalms 91:10
Isaiah 54:17
Matthew 16:19
Psalms 33:12
Psalms 72:17
Psalms 23:6

Chapter III

Prayers for Needs and Special Requests

When You Have a Need or Desire in Your Life

Father, I come before You in prayer, making my petition and request known unto You. Your Word says that if I would ask, I *"shall"* receive. So according to Your Word, I ask that You would bless me with _____.

Father, You told us in Your Word that if we would seek first the Kingdom of God and all of Your righteousness, You would bless our needs and desires to be added (given) unto us. You also said that if we would delight ourselves in You, that You would bless us with the desires of our heart.

Father, I pray that You would help and bless me to always seek You and Your righteousness first in my life. And as I seek Your face, and delight myself in Your Word and in Your ways, I thank You for fulfilling Your Word in my life and blessing me with my heart's desire.

Lord, You are my Shepherd. And as my Shepherd, I confess Your Word that I shall not want (or be in lack of) any good, beneficial, or needful thing in my life. For You are the God of my provisions, who supplies all my needs and desires according to Your riches in glory. For You promised that You would not withhold any good thing from me as I walk upright before You.

Father, You said in Your Word that if I would have faith as a grain of mustard seed, that I could speak to my circumstances and command them to be changed. For You said that those who are redeemed of the Lord can boldly *"say so,"* or confess that it *"is so"* in our lives. So Father, I release my faith in You, and in the awesome power and authority of Your unfailing Word, and I confess and *"say so"* that _____ is manifested in my life, and it shall come to pass.

Father, as I have confessed Your Word concerning _____, I bind every evil spirit that would attempt to stop or hinder me from receiving _____, by my authority in the name of Jesus Christ.

Now Father, this is the confidence that I have in You: That if I ask anything according to Your will, I know that You hear me. And since I know that You hear me (no matter what I ask), then I know that I have received the petition (answered prayer) that I desire, and have asked of You. I believe it, and by faith I receive Your blessing of _____ in my life.

In the name of Jesus Christ, I pray, AMEN!

Scriptures Used In This Prayer:

Philippians 4:6
John 16:24
Matthew 6:33
Psalms 37:4
Psalms 27:8
Psalms 23:1
Psalms 84:11
Philippians 4:19
Matthew 17:20
Psalms 107:2
Matthew 16:19
1 John 5:14
1 John 5:15

For a Test or Exam

Father, I come before You asking for Your help as I prepare to take this exam.

Father, Your Word tells me that the Holy Spirit shall bring all things back to my remembrance. So I'm asking that as I have studied and prepared to take this test, that You would cause all things that I have seen and heard regarding the subjects of this test to come back to my mind. For You said in Your Word that the memory of the *"just"* (those who are born-again) is blessed.

I'm asking that You would help me to think my best, remember my best, and answer the questions to the best of my ability.

Father, I thank You for the spirit of Daniel to be upon me as I take this test. For Your Word says that Daniel was a man with an "Excellent Spirit" who excelled in knowledge, skill, and understanding.

As I prepare to take this test, I pray that You would give me Your divine wisdom. May You lead, guide, and direct me by Your Spirit through every question, and may You give me Your answer of peace concerning every decision.

By the authority of the name of Jesus Christ, I bind and loose fear and nervousness from me. For Your Word tells me that You have not given me a spirit of fear, but of power and of love, and a sound mind.

So I pray that You would give me the mind of Christ—one that is undisturbed, unclouded, and un-distracted by any thoughts, imaginations, or issues. I thank You for also helping me to keep my mind clear and focused on the subjects at hand.

Now Father, I commit this test unto You. For Your Word tells me that You are able to complete and bring to pass the things that I commit to You in prayer. Therefore, I thank You for the results of a good and favorable outcome and score on this test.

In the name of Jesus Christ, I pray. AMEN!

Scriptures Used In This Prayer:

John 14:26
2 Timothy 2:15
Psalms 30:10
Proverbs 10:7
Daniel 5:12
James 1:5
Psalms 32:8
Genesis 41:16
Matthew 16:19
2 Timothy 1:7
1 Corinthians 2:16
2 Timothy 1:12
Jeremiah 29:11
Psalms 35:27

For a Special Event
(Including Sports and Other Events)

Father, I come before You this day praying for Your help and Your blessings to be upon me concerning _____.

I thank You Father that You have not given me a spirit of fear or failure, but a spirit of power, and of love, and of a sound mind. I therefore bind the spirit of fear and intimidation from my life by the authority of the name of Jesus Christ, and I speak boldness upon my life as I prepare for _____.

Father, as Daniel possessed a "Spirit of Excellence" to excel in everything he did, I thank You for also giving me a "Spirit of Excellence" to excel in this _____. And as You anointed Samson with supernatural ability and strength, I pray that You would also anoint me with supernatural strength and ability to succeed.

Father, I know that You do not show favoritism, but I'm asking that You would help me to perform at my maximum ability, and to give my very best and highest effort. Help me to be keen in my thinking, and to be diligent in my performance.

* *(IF IT'S A TEAM EFFORT)* Father, I pray that You would help us as teammates to work together as a team. Keep pride, bad attitudes, strife, and division from among us. May You help us to work together in unity, and be of one mind and of one accord. And, help us as a team to think our best and perform our best together.

Now Father, I commit this _____ unto You. I thank You for Your wisdom, strength, and ability to help me/us to give my/our best effort and performance. And, I release my faith in You, and in Your ability to help and bless me/us to prosper in _____, and to give me/us a favorable outcome.

In the name of Jesus Christ, I pray. AMEN!

Scriptures Used In This Prayer

Hebrews 4:16
2 Timothy 1:7
Matthew 16:19
Daniel 5:12
Judges 15:14-15
Psalms 38:22
1 Corinthians 1:10
Philippians 2:2
Psalms 37:5
Romans 4:21
Psalms 1:3

For Your Tithes and Offerings

F ather, I realize that You are my source, and the source of all my blessings. So I give my tithes and offerings unto You this day as a token of my love and appreciation for You, and for Your love, grace, mercy, and Your blessings upon my life.

You instructed us to bring all the tithes into the storehouse and prove You. So Father, as I give my tithes and my offerings, I thank You for proving Yourself strong in my life with Your (*open*) windows of heaven's blessings.

I confess Your Word that all of my desires and needs are met according to Your riches in glory, and that I have all sufficiency in all things. I also confess Your Word that I am blessed exceedingly, abundantly, and above all that I can ask or think—spiritually, physically, socially, and financially.

Father, because I am a tither and a giver, I also thank You for the rights and privileges You have given unto me to decree Your Word over my life. I therefore decree that I am blessed with strength and continued good health; I am blessed with prosperity and financial increase; I am blessed with success at home and at school; and I am also blessed with success in special events and activities. Father, because of Your favor, I declare that increase and blessings are upon every area my life. And I decree that I am also blessed to prosper in everything I do, and in every aspect of my life.

As I give my tithes and my offerings, I thank You for blessing them to be multiplied and given back unto me—a good measure, pressed down, shaken together, and running over shall You cause them to be returned unto me from the north, south, east, and west.

Now Father, as I commit my tithes and my offerings to You, I receive the promise of Your blessings upon my life. And I speak Your Word that no evil spirit shall be able to hinder, delay, or stop Your blessings upon my life in any way.

In the name of the Lord, Jesus Christ, I pray. AMEN!

Scriptures Used In This Prayer:

2 Corinthians 9:6-7
Malachi 3:10
Philippians 4:19
2 Corinthians 9:8
Ephesians 3:20
Job 22:28
Deuteronomy 28:1-13
Luke 6:38
Isaiah 43:5-6
Malachi 3:11
Psalms 37:5
Isaiah 54:17

Chapter IV

Prayers for Salvation, Spiritual Growth, and Strength

A Prayer of Salvation
(A Sinner's Prayer)

Father, I come before You confessing that I am a sinner in need of salvation. Father, according to Your Word, I confess that Jesus Christ is the Son of the living God, and He died on the cross and shed His blood for my sins. I ask that You would forgive me of my sins and my life of sin; create within me a clean heart, and give me a mind, will, desire, and heart to serve, please, and obey You.

Now Satan, I denounce you as the lord and controller of my life, and I evict you from my life and my heart. Lord Jesus, I now open my heart to You. I ask that You would come into my heart and make Your abode. Father, I ask that You would lead me by Your Word and by Your Spirit, and help me to live a life that is pleasing in Your sight.

Now Father, by Your mercy and grace, and by faith in Your Word, I receive my salvation and my eternal life through the blood of Jesus Christ. And I stand in faith that my salvation is sealed unto the day of redemption, and cannot be taken away.

In the name of Jesus Christ, I thank You, I give You praise, and I receive my salvation. AMEN!

Scriptures Used In This Prayer:

Romans 1:16
2 Corinthians 7:10
Matthew 16:16
Hebrews 9:11-15
1 John 1:9
Psalms 51:1-10
Romans 10:8-10
Romans 8:9
Romans 8:14
Colossians 1:10-11
Ephesians 2:13
1 Peter 1:18-21
Psalms 19:14
Ephesians 4:30

For Someone to Receive Salvation

This prayer may be used for an individual person or a group of people, such as your family, friends, peers or schoolmates.

Father, I thank You for sending Your Son, Jesus Christ, so that the lost of the world could be saved. For You said that You are not slack concerning Your promise, but patient towards us, and not willing that any would perish and miss out on Your gift of eternal life, but that all would come to repentance. Therefore, I pray for _____ that You would save _____ and bring _____ to Your salvation.

Father, I pray that You would place faithful laborers of the Gospel in _____'s path. I pray that everywhere _____ turns, that _____ would meet someone who is a bold witness for You, sharing and declaring the Gospel of Jesus Christ with _____.

Instead of _____ being influenced by Satan and by the world to resist and rebel against Your ways, I thank You for the influence of Your Spirit to be upon _____ instead. May You pierce _____'s heart by Your spirit with conviction, and give _____ a mind and a heart to receive You and Your salvation through Your Word.

Father, even as Jesus Christ called forth Lazarus from the dead and commanded that he be loosed and set free, I call forth _____ from spiritual death and bondage into the marvelous light and salvation of Jesus Christ. I command _____'s heart, mind and soul to be loosed and set free from every stronghold and hindrance of _____'s salvation, by the authority of the name of Jesus Christ. For he in whom the Son has set free, is free indeed!

By my authority in the name of Jesus Christ, I bind every evil spirit that has blinded _____'s mind and heart from receiving Christ. I therefore loose _____'s mind to see that _____ needs Christ, and _____'s heart to become open and receptive to receive Jesus as Savior and Lord.

Now Father, as I have prayed Your Word over _____'s life, I release my faith in the power of Your Word to save _____ and set _____ free from every hindrance of _____'s salvation. And, as I have interceded for _____'s salvation, I speak those things that be not as though they were, and I confess that _____ is saved and born-again.

In the name of Jesus Christ, I pray. AMEN!

Scriptures Used In This Prayer:

1 John 4:10
2 Peter 3:9
Luke 10:2
Ephesians 6:19
Romans 12:2
Luke 24:47
Acts 4:12
John 11:43-44
John 8:36
Matthew 16:19
Acts 10:36
Matthew 18:11
Romans 4:17

For A Closer Walk with the Lord

Heavenly Father, I come before You this day asking that You would help me to have a closer walk with You.

Father, Your Word says that if I would draw near to You, that You would draw near to me. So I'm asking that You would help me to press towards You and draw near to You. And as I do so, I thank You for also drawing near to me—keeping me close to You, and in Your secret place.

Father, even as You love us, and Your love is constantly renewed for us each day, I'm asking that You would also help me to keep my love renewed for You. Help me to love You with all of my heart, soul, strength, and might. I pray that You would keep my heart in Your precious love, and not allow anything to separate me from You, or my love from You.

Father, I'm asking that You would give me a continuing hunger, thirst, and desire for Your presence in my life. Give me a heart to praise, worship, and exalt You each day, and give me a hunger and a desire to read, study, confess, and obey Your Word.

I'm asking that You would give me a praying spirit. Help me to be a young man/woman of prayer—who prays daily, not only for my life, but also for my family and for others.

I'm asking that You would keep me from becoming lukewarm or conformed to the world. Instead, keep me on fire for You, and give me a heart and a passion to love, serve, and obey You in all things.

By my authority in the name of Jesus Christ, I bind every demonic spirit that would try to stop or hinder my spiritual life or spiritual growth. I loose every weight and power of darkness from my life. I also bind and loose every evil spirit that would try to separate me from God. For I declare that nothing shall be able to separate me from the love of God, through Christ Jesus, our Lord.

Now Father, as I have prayed Your Word, I thank You that Your Word is established in my heart and in my life. And I thank You for keeping me close to You in Your love, and in Your presence all the days of my life.

In the name of Jesus Christ, I pray. AMEN!

Scriptures Used In This Prayer:

Hebrews 4:16
James 4:8
Philippians 3:14
Psalms 91:1
Ephesians 4:23
Mark 12:30
Romans 8:35
Romans 8:38-39
Matthew 5:6
2 Timothy 2:15
James 1:22
James 5:16
Revelation 3:16
Romans 12:2
2 Corinthians 2:9
Matthew 16:19
Hebrews 12:1
Romans 8:39
Psalms 23:6

To Be an Effective Witness

F ather, I come before Your throne of grace that I may find the boldness, faith, and strength I need to be an effective witness and soul winner for the Kingdom of God.

I pray first of all, that You would help me to let the light of Jesus Christ shine through my ways, my words, my actions, and every aspect of my life. May You cause my life to be such a living and effective witness through the light of Christ, that my family, friends, peers, and others around me may see my light, and be drawn to Jesus Christ through me.

I pray that You would help me to be led by Your Spirit. May You lead me to whom I should witness, and give me the right timing to witness. As I open my mouth to share Christ, I pray that You would give me the right scriptures, illustrations, and examples to effectively convey Christ to them and win them over unto You. And may You also prepare their hearts to be open and receptive to the words that I speak.

Father, You said in Your Word that the righteous are as bold as a lion. I pray therefore for boldness in my life to speak Your Word and testify of Jesus Christ. Help me to boldly—without shame, fear, embarrassment, or intimidation, share the Gospel of Christ.

I bind every spirit of fear and shame in my heart to share Christ. I confess the Word of God that I am not ashamed in any way of the Gospel of Christ; for it is the power of God to bring salvation to others. I also confess Your Word that You have not given me a spirit of fear (to witness), but of power, love, and a bold and sound mind.

Now Father, I thank You for Godly boldness and wisdom in my witness, and for Your power and anointing upon me to be an effective and successful soul winner for the Kingdom of God. And I pray that You would use my witness to draw my family, friends, schoolmates, and peers unto the Kingdom of God and unto Your salvation.

In the name of the Lord, Jesus Christ I pray. AMEN!

Scriptures Used In This Prayer:

Hebrews 4:16
Acts 1:8
Matthew 5:16
Romans 8:14
Proverbs 16:3
Psalms 25:5
Exodus 31:3
Jeremiah 9:20
Proverbs 28:1
Matthew 16:19
Romans 1:16
2 Timothy 1:7
Mark 16:15
2 Corinthians 5:11
2 Corinthians 6:2
Hebrews 3:15

Chapter V

Prayers for Physical and Emotional Healing

For Healing

F ather, I come boldly before Your throne of grace confessing Your Word concerning my healing.

Father, You have revealed Yourself to us through Your Word as *Jehovah Rapha*—the Lord God who heals me, and removes sickness and disease from my body. So I thank You for removing this infirmity from me.

Father, You said in Your Word that You desire above all things for me that I would prosper and have good health. So I thank You for prospering me in my healing, and restoring good health unto my body. For You said that healing is the children's (children of God) bread. I am a child of God; therefore, healing and good health belong to me.

Father, by my faith in You, and by the authority of Your Word, I confess that the Lord Jesus Christ was wounded for my transgressions; He was bruised for my iniquities; the chastisement of my peace was upon Him, and I decree and declare according to the

Word of the living God, that *"WITH HIS STRIPES, I AM HEALED!"*

I thank You for redeeming me by the blood of the lamb, Jesus Christ. For You said to let the redeemed of the Lord begin to *say so*. Father, I am the redeemed of the Lord, and I boldly *"say so"* that I am healed from the crown of my head to the soles of my feet!

By my authority in Christ Jesus, I bind this spirit of sickness and disease from my body, and I loose it from me. I decree that this weapon of sickness that has been formed against my body can no longer prosper. I decree that this weapon of sickness must cease, now! I also decree by my authority in Christ that my healing begin taking place and become manifested in my body.

Now Father, You said in Your Word that the effectual, fervent prayers of a child of God will prevail in victory. So, as I have prayed Your Word over my body, I release my faith in the power and authority of Your Word to bring my healing to pass. So Father, I stand upon Your Word as I decree once again, *"WITH THE STRIPES OF JESUS CHRIST, I AM HEALED!"* AMEN!

Scriptures Used In This Prayer:

Hebrews 4:16
Exodus 15:26
Exodus 23:25
3 John 1:2
Proverbs 6:30-31
Matthew 15:26
Isaiah 53:5
1 Peter 2:24
Titus 2:14
Psalms 107:2
Matthew 16:19
Isaiah 54:17
Job 22:28
James 5:16
Isaiah 53:5

When You Have Been Hurt or Disappointed

Heavenly Father, I come boldly before Your throne of grace that I may find and obtain help, strength, and encouragement in a time of need.

Father, I confess that I have been hurt/ disappointed because of (*what happened*). But I know that in times like these, I can look unto You for my help. For Your Word says that You are a very present help in times of trouble, and I can run unto You (in prayer) where there is strength and encouragement.

I ask according to Your Word for forgiveness for (*person who offended You*) for (*name the offense*). For Your Word commands us to pray for and forgive those who offend us and do us wrong.

Father, Your Word says that You came to heal the broken hearted and bind up our wounds. So as I have been hurt by this affliction, I pray that You would bind up the wounds of this hurt, and heal my heart by the comfort and strength of Your Spirit.

As I go through this affliction, help me to keep my

mind and heart upon You. For You said that You would keep us in Your perfect peace, as we keep our minds and hearts stayed upon You.

Father, Your Word says that You are the lifter of our heads (the one who lifts us up in times of sadness, despair and discouragement). Your Word also says that You are our joy and gladness in times of sorrow. I thank You therefore that as You renew the strength of the eagle, that You would cause my heart to be uplifted, and my joy and gladness renewed and restored, through the strength of Your Spirit and the power of Your Word.

By my authority in Christ Jesus, I bind every spirit of depression, oppression, and any other spirit that the enemy would try to put on me as a result of this adversity. I loose them from my mind and my heart, and I render them powerless to keep me sad, bewildered, or depressed, by the authority of the name of Jesus Christ!

Now Father, I thank You for Your comfort and strength, and for the restoration of my soul. And as I have prayed and spoken Your Word over my life, I thank You that sadness, despair, and depression is rebuked and removed from my mind and my heart. I confess that I am now healed, restored, encouraged, and strengthened by Your Spirit, and I now walk in my joy in You, O Lord—which is my strength, and my victory in Christ Jesus.

In the name of the Lord, Jesus Christ, I pray, AMEN!

Scriptures Used In This Prayer:

Hebrews 4:16
Psalms 121:1
Psalms 121:2
Psalms 46:1
Proverbs 18:10
Luke 11:4
Matthew 5:44
Isaiah 61:1
Isaiah 26:3
Psalms 3:3
Isaiah 40:31
Nehemiah 8:10
Matthew 16:19
Psalms 23:3
Malachi 3:11
Colossians 1:11
Nehemiah 8:10

Chapter VI

Prayers for Safety and Directions

A Prayer Of The 23rd Psalm
A Psalm of God's Comfort, Peace And Provisions

O Lord, my God, You are my Shepherd. And because You are, You supply all of my needs according to Your riches in glory in Christ.

Lord, because You are my Shepherd, You are the One who loves me, cares for me, and provide what I need. You also cause me to be covered in Your grace, and to lie down in the green pastures of Your abundant blessings.

Whatever problems or difficulties I face in life, You are always with me, leading me beside the still waters of your peace and serenity.

You are the restorer of my soul. When I am weak, You give me strength; when I am hurt, You encourage my heart and pick me up; and when I am sad or lonely, You comfort me and give me joy.

You lead in the path of Your righteousness (right living) and obedience to Your Word, for Your name's sake.

When I go through valleys in my life of troubles

and trials, I will not fear, worry or fret, because I know that You are my Great Shepherd, and You said that You will never leave nor forsake me, and You will always see me through.

As my Shepherd, You lead and guide me by the rod of Your Word and the staff of Spirit and authority. You teach me Your laws and Your ways, and You bring correction to me when I am wrong. For You are the One who reproves me through the Your Spirit, and the convicting power of Your Word.

Because You are my Shepherd, when adverse situations and trouble come against me, You are always there with me. You prepare a table of Your favor, peace and blessings for me in the presence of those who are against me.

You fill me with Your presence and Your anointing, and it breaks and destroys every yoke and hindrance of the devil in my life.

You are a faithful God, and a faithful Shepherd over my life. And because of Your faithfulness, You cause Your abounding love to follow me all the days of my life, and You cause Your goodness, mercy, and loving kindness to overflow in my life.

And because You are my good Shepherd, I shall dwell and abide in You, in Your presence, and under Your arms of comfort, peace and provisions, both now and forever, AMEN!

Scriptures Used In This Prayer:

Psalms Chapter 23

For Safety and Protection

F ather, I come before Your throne of grace asking for Your divine safety and protection in my life.

I confess Your Word that You are my refuge and my fortress. You are my God in whom I put my trust to keep me safe.

I thank You for assigning strong and mighty angels to be encamped in a hedge around my life. I thank You that they are on guard continually to watch over me and protect me from all accidents, hurt, harm, and danger.

I confess Your Word that no evil can come upon me, and no danger can even come near me, my home, or my surroundings.

I confess the Word of God over my life that no weapon (spiritual or physical) that is formed against me can prosper. I also confess that the Lord rebukes every evil attack against my life.

Father, I ask that You would not only protect my

life, but that You would also protect my parents and all of my family. May You watch over each of us daily, and keep us in Your secret place—under the shadow of Your protection and safety.

By the authority of the name of Jesus Christ, I bind and loose every evil spirit that would attempt to cause harm or injury to my life, or to the lives of my family. I confess, according to the Word of God, that I am an anointed child of God; therefore, Satan is rebuked from my life and from my family, and he cannot touch or harm us in any way.

Father, I confess Your Word that since I am a Christian, then You are with me. And since You are, then no spirit, force, or person is able to come against my life or the lives of my family and succeed.

Now Father, I commit my life, and the lives of my family unto Your hands. And I am confident that as I have prayed Your Word, that You are able to watch over us and keep us safe this day, and all the days of our lives.

In the name of the Lord Jesus Christ, I pray. AMEN!

Scriptures Used In This Prayer:

Psalms 91:2
Psalms 91:11-12
Psalms 91:10
Isaiah 54:17
Malachi 3:11
Psalms 91:1-2
Matthew 16:19
1 Chronicles 16:22
Romans 8:31
Psalms 17:8
Psalms 140:4

When You are Fearful or Afraid

Father, I come boldly before Your throne of grace to find encouragement and help in a time of need from fear.

I thank You Father for blessing and allowing me to dwell in Your secret place, and abide under Your Almighty shadow of protection. I say of You, O Lord, that You are my Refuge and my Fortress. You are also my God in whom I trust to protect and keep me.

I confess Your Word that You have not given me a spirit of fear, but a spirit of power, and of love, and a sound mind.

I thank You for assigning strong and mighty angels to watch over me. I thank You for encamping them in a hedge of protection around me to fight for me, guard me, protect me, keep me in all my ways, and deliver me from all dangers and afflictions.

Father, I confess Your Word that since You are my light and my salvation, I have no need to fear. And since You are the strength of my life, I have no need to be afraid. Therefore, I choose not to walk in fear, but in the confidence of Your ability to protect me and keep me safe.

I thank You for the power and the authority You have given me through Christ Jesus. And with that authority, I bind every principality and every evil spirit from my life. I decree that no weapon (physical or spiritual) that is formed against me can prosper in any way. I also decree that they are helpless, powerless, inoperative and ineffective against me.

I thank You for keeping me in Your peace—the peace that passes all understanding. And I pray that You would help me to keep my heart and mind continually in Your peace and stayed upon You.

Now Father, I rest in this confidence: Knowing that since You are with me, then nothing is strong enough or able to come against me and succeed. I therefore give You praise and thanksgiving for my complete safety, for my deliverance from fear, and for Your divine protection upon my life.

In the name of Jesus Christ I pray, AMEN!

Scriptures Used In This Prayer

Psalms 91:1-2
2 Timothy 1:7
Psalms 91:11-12
Psalms 127:1
Matthew 16:19
Job 22:28
Isaiah 54:17
Isaiah 26:3
Romans 8:31
Psalms 4:8

For Guidance and Direction

F ather, I come before You this day asking for Your guidance and direction in my life concerning _____.

Your Word says that if I would acknowledge You in my ways that You would direct my path. As I must make a decision concerning _____, I seek Your face and acknowledge You for Your guidance and direction.

Father, You promised to give us the Comforter, which is the Holy Spirit. For You said that the Holy Spirit shall lead and guide us in all things. I thank You Father that I am filled with the Holy Spirit. And as I need to make this decision, I thank You that it's the Holy Spirit within me that shall lead and guide me in the right direction.

Father, You know all things. Your Word says that You even know the end results of a thing before it actually begins. I pray therefore, since You already know the outcome, that You would lead and guide me with Your eyes and Your Spirit in the right path.

For You said that You would guide us with Your eyes and order our footsteps.

I confess Your Word that You are my shepherd. And as a shepherd guides his sheep, I thank You for also guiding me in the right path and direction that I need to take. I speak the Word of God that I shall not be deceived into listening to, or being lead by the wrong voice (the voice of the stranger—Satan), but I shall clearly hear, listen to, and be guided only by the voice of my Great Shepherd, Jesus Christ.

By my authority in Christ, I bind and loose every demonic spirit that the enemy would attempt to use against me to deceive me. I cast down every spirit of deception, and every trick of Satan that would try to hinder me from making the right and godly choice and decision.

Now Father, I cast all my cares upon You concerning this decision that I must make. And I thank You in advance for divinely speaking to my heart, giving me Your answer of peace, and guiding me in the right path.

In the name of Jesus Christ, I pray. AMEN!

Scriptures Used In This Prayer

Hebrews 4:16
Proverbs 3:6
Luke 12:12
John 14:26
Psalms 1:6
Psalms 94:11
Revelation 1:8
Psalms 32:8
Psalms 37:23
Psalms 23:1
John 10:4-5
Matthew 16:19
2 Corinthians 10:5
Psalms 55:22
1 Peter 5:7
Genesis 41:16
Psalms 23:3

A Prayer at Bedtime
(For Safe, Restful, and Sound Sleep)

Heavenly Father, as I prepare to lie down to sleep tonight, I want to thank You and praise You for Your love and kindness today. I thank You for Your provisions this day, and for protecting me, and blessing me with Your many wonderful blessings upon my life.

Father, You said in Your Word that You give the children of God "*sweet sleep*." So therefore, I ask according to Your Word for sweet, sound, and restful sleep tonight. And I thank You for also giving me peaceful and pleasant dreams.

Father, if I have sinned against You or disobeyed Your Word today, I ask that You would have mercy upon me according to Your loving kindness and tender mercy, and forgive me for the wrongs that I have done. I not only ask that You would forgive me for my sins, but I also ask that You would forgive anyone who may have sinned against me or wronged me in any way.

In the name of Jesus Christ, I bind and loose every evil spirit from my sleep and my dreams. And I speak the Word of God that no evil spirit shall be able to come upon me, nor shall they be able to hinder my sleep, disturb my rest, or infiltrate my dreams in any way.

Father, even as You have safely protected me and guided me through this day, I commit my life unto You to also safely take me through this night.

As the morning comes, I thank You for waking me up well refreshed and rested in my mind and my body. I thank You for also waking me up prepared to pray, and prepared to serve You and live for You throughout the coming day.

In the name of the Jesus Christ, I pray. AMEN.

Scriptures Used In This Prayer:

Psalms 113:3	Matthew 16:19
Psalms 92:1	Psalms 91:5
Psalms 127:2	Psalms 91:10
Psalms 4:8	Psalms 37:5
Proverbs 3:24	Psalms 118:24
1 John 1:9	
Psalms 51:1	

Chapter VII

Prayers for Spiritual Help, Deliverance, and Forgiveness

To Stand Against Peer Pressure

F ather, I come before You this day asking for Your help to stand against peer pressure and temptation.

Father, I thank You for keeping me from being influenced or persuaded to compromise with my friends or peers to commit sin, wrong, or evil. Instead, I pray that You would cause me to be influenced only by the Holy Spirit within me to do that which is right, good, and pleasing unto You.

I thank You Father for giving me the mind of Christ. And, even as Christ resisted and did not heed to the temptations of Satan, I thank You for also empowering me with the mind and will of Christ to resist peer pressure and temptations. I thank You for not only keeping me from heeding to the temptations of peer pressure, but may You also keep me from being seduced and influenced by the negative influences of television, movies, and music.

Father, help me not to be influenced or blinded by Satan to belittle or look down upon my Christian life.

Help me not to see my Christian life as being boring or incomplete. Instead, help me to see my life as totally complete in You. I pray that You would also help me to delight myself in You, Your ways, and Your Word. And help me to walk in my joy in You, O Lord, which is my strength.

Lord, I confess Your Word that I am not ashamed of the Gospel of Christ in any way. I also confess that You have not given me a spirit of fear, shame, or timidity in my Christian walk. But instead, You have given me a spirit of power and boldness in my testimony of Jesus Christ, and in my Christian convictions and ethics.

By my authority in the name of Jesus Christ, I bind and loose every evil influence from my life, and I cast down every wicked and demonic imagination from my heart and mind.

Now Father, I stand upon Your Word which says that You are able to keep me from falling. And I speak Your Word, that greater is Jesus Christ who is in me, (who is able to strengthen me and keep me from falling to temptation and peer pressure), than the enemy that is in the world.

In the name of Jesus Christ, I pray. AMEN!

Scriptures Used In This Prayer:

Hebrews 4:16
Acts 13:43
Romans 14:5
Romans 12:2
Ephesians 5:18
1 John 3:22
1 Corinthians 2:16
2 Corinthians 4:4
Colossians 2:10
Psalms 37:4
Galatians 5:16
Nehemiah 8:10
Romans 1:16
2 Timothy 1:7
Acts 4:29
Acts 4:31
Matthew 16:19
2 Corinthians 10:4-5
1 John 5:4
Romans 8:37
Jude 1:24
1 John 4:4
Exodus 15:2

To Overcome Temptations and Strongholds

May also be used to overcome bad and evil habits or addictions, such as drugs, smoking, drinking, etc.

Father, I come boldly before Your throne of grace to find help, strength, and deliverance in a time of need. You said that if we ask anything according to Your will, that You will hear us and answer us. Therefore, I ask that You would deliver me from the temptation/problem of _____.

I pray that You would lead me away from the temptation of _____, and deliver me from it. Give me Your strength, mind, and will to resist _____ when I am tempted, and give me Your wisdom to avoid places, things, and people that would tempt, lure, or lead me to _____.

I thank You Father that the weapons of our warfare are not carnal, but mighty through You, O God, to the pulling down of strongholds and casting down imaginations. Therefore, by the authority of the Word of God, I pull down this stronghold of _____ in my life. I loose its power and influence over me, and I break the yoke of _____ in my life, by the authority of the name of Jesus Christ.

Father, I confess Your Word that I am crucified with Christ. I also confess that my old life and nature of sin have also been crucified. And the life that I now live, I live it by the faith, power, and strength of Christ—who gives me the strength and power to overcome _____. I also speak Your Word that I am now more than a conqueror over _____ because of my victory through Jesus Christ, my Lord.

I thank You Father for Your help—that from this day forward, that I walk in the light and power of my redemption and deliverance which You gave me when Jesus died on the Cross. And I decree that I am loosed and set free from _____. For he in whom the Son has set free (through the power of Your Word) is free indeed.

Now Father, I thank You for setting me free and delivering me from every evil work and power of darkness of _____. I therefore walk in this liberty, and I stand steadfast and unmovable in my place of victory in Christ. I now receive my victory and deliverance. For greater is Jesus Christ who lives and dwells within me (who gives me power over _____), than the enemy who is in the world.

In the name of Jesus Christ, I pray, AMEN!

Scriptures Used In This Prayer:

Hebrews 4:16
1 John 5:14-15
Matthew 6:13
Psalms 91:3
Nehemiah 8:10
2 Samuel 22:33
1 Corinthians
James 4:7
1 Corinthians 10:13
Hebrews 4:15
James 1:13-15
Romans 12:21
1 John 2:13-14
1 Thessalonians 5:22
2 Corinthians 10:4

Isaiah 58:6
Galatians 2:20
Romans 8:37
1 John 5:4
Psalms 121:1-3
1 John 1:7
Ephesians 6:10
Job 22:28
Matthew 16:19
John 8:36
2 Timothy 4:18
Galatians 5:1
1 Corinthians 15:57-58
1 John 4:4

When You Have Sinned
(and for Power Over Sin and Temptation)

F ather, I come before You this day asking for Your forgiveness for my sins and disobedience.

Father, Your Word says that if I would confess my sins (unto You), that You are faithful and merciful to forgive me of my sins and cleanse me from all of my unrighteousness.

I therefore repent before You, and I confess that I have *(name what You have done)*. Lord, I am sorry for disobeying You, and I ask for Your mercy, grace, and Your forgiveness.

Father, as I have confessed my sins, I ask that You would have mercy upon me according to Your loving-kindness, and according to the multitude of Your tender mercy, blot out my sins and transgressions, and cover them with the precious blood of Jesus Christ—that they be remembered no more.

I thank You for giving me the mind of Christ. I ask that You would give me Your mind, strength, and will to resist this sin and temptation in the future, and any other temptation or sin that Satan would try to use to tempt or lure me.

I confess Your Word that I abide in Christ, and He abides in me. And therefore, greater is Jesus Christ who is in me, who gives me power over sin and temptation, than Satan who temps me to do wrong or evil.

By my authority in Christ, I bind and loose Satan, and the spirit of disobedience, sin, and rebellion from my life. And I confess the Word of God that I am strong in the Lord, Jesus Christ, and in the power of His might to resist temptation, disobedience, and sin.

Now Father, I believe by faith according to Your Word that as I have confessed my sins and wrongs, that You have forgiven me, and the blood of Jesus Christ has cleansed me from them. I also confess Your Word that I am now strengthened and established in Your Word, and in Your power to keep me from falling. In the name of Jesus Christ, I pray. AMEN!

Scriptures Used In This Prayer:

1 John 1:9	Mark 6:7
Psalms 51:1	Matthew 16:19
1 Corinthians 2:16	Ephesians 6:10
James 4:7	Colossians 2:6-7
John 15:4	Jude 1:24
1 John 4:4	

For Power Over Lust and Sexual Temptation

Father, I come before You this day asking for Your help to deliver me from sexual temptation.

Father, I speak Your Word over my life that I am a young man/woman of God, and I am crucified with Christ; therefore, the lusts of my flesh have also been crucified. I confess that Christ lives in me, and I now live my life by my faith in Christ, and His strength and power working in and through me.

Lord, I pray that You would lead me away from the temptation of my flesh. And may You strengthen and deliver me from every trap and snare of lust, pornography, and every manner of sexual sin, immorality and temptation.

Father, I thank You for giving me the mind of Christ. I thank You also for giving me Your strength and will to resist Satan and sexual sins and temptations. For You said in Your Word that if I would resist the devil, he would flee from me.

Help me not to compromise or be influenced by

my friends, peers, or the wrong crowd to give *in* to sin or sexual immorality. I pray that You would also keep me from being drawn to sexual sins and temptations through negative television programs, movies or music. Instead, help me to stand steadfast and unmovable in my faith in You and in Your power to keep me from falling.

By the authority I have in Christ Jesus, I bind and loose every spirit of lust, and every influence of sexual sin and bondage from my mind and my life. And I confess that I walk in the spirit, and I will not give in to, nor fulfill any of the lusts of the flesh or the lust of the eyes in any way.

Father, Your Word says that You are able to keep us from evil, and deliver us from temptation. So as I have prayed Your Word, I confess that I shall stand strong in You, O Lord, and in the power of Your might, and I shall walk in my victory in Christ Jesus.

In the name of the Lord, Jesus Christ, I pray. AMEN.

Scriptures Used In This Prayer

Proverbs 2:16
Galatians 2:20
Matthew 6:13
Psalms 28:7
Psalms 91:3
Psalms 101:3
1 Corinthians 2:16
James 4:7
Matthew 26:41
1 Corinthians 15:58
Jude 1:24
Matthew 16:19
Galatians 5:16
1 Chronicles 4:10
1 Corinthians 10:13
Hebrews 2:8
Ephesians 6:10
1 John 5:4

Other Books and Materials
By Kenneth Scott

The Weapons Of Our Warfare, Volume 1

The Weapons Of Our Warfare, Volume 2

The Weapons Of Our Warfare, Volume 3
— Confessing God's Word Over Your Life.

The Weapons Of Our Warfare, Volume 5
— The Warfare of Worship

Volumes 1, 2, 3, Books on CD
(Sold Separately)

When All Hell Breaks Loose

Understanding Your Divine Authority In Prayer

Understanding The Lord's Prayer
— The Basics of Prayer

Standing In The Gap

The Warfare of Fasting

Chains the Bind Generations
(Deliverances From Generational Curses)

The Warfare of Intercession

Why We act Like That

The Witchcraft of profanity

For other available materials, visit us on the web at:

www.prayerwarfare.com

Contact Us:

For prayer requests, questions or comments, write to:

Spiritual Warfare Ministries
Attention: Kenneth Scott
P.O. Box 2024
Birmingham, Alabama 35201-2024

(205) 853-9509

Web Site: www.prayerwarfare.com

email us at prayerbooks@aol.com

This book is not available in all bookstores. To order additional copies of this book, please send $10.99 plus $2.98 shipping and handling to the above address.

God has anointed Pastor Scott to teach and preach on the power of prayer. If you are interested in him coming to minister at your church or organization, please contact him at the information above.

Printed in Great Britain
by Amazon